BOOK FOR JOHN

Poems by Edward Bartók-Baratta

BOOK FOR JOHN
© 2008 Edward Bartók-Baratta. All rights reserved. No part of this book may
be used or reproduced in any manner whatsoever, except in the case of brief
quotations embedded in critical articles and reviews.

MotherJill Press

ISBN: 0-9778073-0-4
Library of Congress cataloging data in progress

10 9 8 7 6 5 4 3 2 1

Poems from *Book for John* appear in these publications:

African American Review, "Kevin's Body";
Artful Dodge, "The Sleepers," "This Solitude," "Whose Turn Is It";
Ascent, "Father";
Brilliant Corners, "The American House of Jazz and Poetry";
Confrontation, "Bringing the Dog Back," "Dead Boys";
Denver Quarterly, "Priests in a Car," "A Seed Found in an Old Book of Poems";
Image, "Drive," "Witness";
The Laurel Review, "Notes of a Great Executive";
LIT, "The Name";
Manoa: A Pacific Journal of International Writing, "Lemonade," "This Place, Now";
Many Mountains Moving, "As You Eat Eggs";
The Massachusetts Review, "Lullaby";
Mid-American Review, "No, Edward";
Mudfish, "Who Else but The Ice Man";
New Orleans Review, "A Goodbye to the Great Susannah McCorkle";
Northeast Corridor, "What There Was";
Northwest Florida Review, "The History of Baseball";
Ploughshares, "Prenuptial";
Plum Review, "The Complete Works";
Poets Respond to Violence in America, anthology, University of Iowa Press, "The Men Who Killed My Brother";
River Styx, "Fire Escape";
Salt Hill, "3:15";
Seattle Review, "Boy Who Cried Wolf," "Near and Distant Neighbors";
Seneca Review, "Immigration";
Southern Poetry Review, "Be Not Afraid";
Spoon River Poetry Review, "Why Don't the Children Call Anymore";
Steve, (an Italian review, in translation, Modena, Italy), "My Love for You";
Sycamore Review, "Dear Carol," "Dear Thomas," "Dialectic";
Verse, (also in *Jacket*, Australia), "The Girl, the Dog, and the Book";
The Virginia Quarterly Review, "In the Night," "Mother and Father Fire";
Willow Review, "Exiled from New Jersey," "Notes on Our Beastly Nature."

I

I know that people will come to me and say, That title makes no sense, Eddie, *Book for John*. They'll say, These poems aren't about that, your brother, his death, or even his life. These poems aren't about any one thing really, they're not a cohesive whole the way they teach poets to make a book in college or the university. During this, I, the writer, the brother, will be looking down at my shoes, because one has to look somewhere, and I'll be thinking something like, Yeah, you people are right, the only thing that holds this book together is that it is a selection of poems chosen from hundreds that I had to write during the fifteen years after a man I love was murdered.

For Aleya. All Peace & Blessings.
Sacred Elder Samara ~ Northampton ~ September 14, 2014

BOOK FOR JOHN
(Poems 1985 – 2000)

CONTENTS   Part One

BOOK FOR JOHN
(Poems 1985 – 2000)

CONTENTS   Part Two

BOOK FOR JOHN

(Poems 1985 - 2000)

IMMIGRATION

This is the country where they murder your brother,
my sister's shoes were broken into here,
the thieves taking both her feet and her left leg
up to the knee. Broken light bulbs were also used
to shave her underarms and eyebrows. The bedside fire
finally did drive her insane. This cage here belonged
to the second brother, the one they allowed to live,
the stains in the corner and the yellowed sheet
like a page in the corner of an old book
where he relieved himself. Living in this way
still he was able to gather sixty years
into his small basket. He disturbed not one twig
when he died. The tank, the thin pin, the earring
that belonged to a hand grenade, masquerading here
as sewing needles, a thimble, a station wagon. This
room with the large table, primarily used for torture,
was also where one received food, yet at times
the hallway served best to buffer the calls
and the screams in the afternoon. Neighbors' doors
bolted from within, a foolproof system. These
two—you'll see that their portraits have held up well
over time, the eyes still following as we approach
the desk—they ordered, oversaw, and carried out
most executions and sentences themselves,
it being our job to assume responsibility, adopt
the guilt for punishment received, and it was demanded
that we express our affection and our undying love,
as well as to address them as Mother and Father. You,
of course, will have to show mastery of the material,
if what you want is to become a citizen here.

Part One, I

PRENUPTIAL

Words, together we'll have
the wedding feast, I'll spread

the canopy, bring the glass
for you to crush. You'll

arrive early, *time* and *light*
in your pocket, dark boxes

in the car, each with the name
of an object. Alone this way,

no guests expected—jars, bottles,
vials with things like *knife*,

cloud, and *blood*. Leave it
until later—to unpack

Sister carefully, in a wire-mesh
glass case, *Mother, Father*

pockmarked inside a dry
mahogany box. Other days,

journey in the distance, not one
verb in the house. Nothing

to compare, question, or qualify
love, ice, blue jay, hell.

DEAR CAROL,

What a stupid anchor my thoughts and feelings
yesterday, I dragged myself around
like I was a punishment somebody gave me,
like I was dressed in nothing but my shorts

and had to stand on the sewer in my old backyard
in front of everybody I knew, making me
a small, unknown thing to myself, dragging myself
away like a man full of whiskey, my heart

polluted, sluggish, dead like my home city,
my fingers fat and incapable of loving. I could've
painted you as you were yesterday, or hired
a harpist to surround you with a song, yet

not while I was on such unspeakable terms
with myself, and you were a stranger to me.

DEAR THOMAS,

The apprenticeship was long and varied:
we carved wooden fruit from necessary furniture.

We learned that a cathedral could have two ceilings:
the one you see, and the one that falls around you.

If our early thoughts were stiff as cardboard,
so were our self-portraits as thin as stickmen.

An invitation to a wedding meant prolific sewing,
how precious to us were those hours of daylight.

A crowd of fools lined up outside our fine school
to audition to be our best friends for life:

we chose them all. Of the early years,
we would change nothing: a dog

to stroke in the dire moonlight, a fig tree
to lead you to a sweetheart's window.

AS YOU EAT EGGS

The hard rain comes, and ants stretch themselves,
they lie prone over the holes of their home—

the egg-shaped dome risen from the earth,
pine needles they collect one at a time.

Lettuce leaves fall under the sun at noon,
large bees come knocking at the cabin window.

The fly has had his seven weeks of life,
then dies trapped between the screen and the wood.

Far north from war, the secluded forest,
a small brown spider walks across the page.

Bombs are dropping on someone else's home.
The eggs of their misfortune are hatching.

WHOSE TURN IS IT

Stand, each of you who has in your closet
a basketball that needs some air. Begin to dance,

all who have unpaid debt. Hum for me
the melody, what's left of your grandmother's song. Step outside

after midnight: wake every dog on the block
when you scream at the top of your lungs

the name of someone you loved
when you were seventeen. Tell us what it is,

in the humid summer night, June bugs
crackling beneath our slippers and our naked feet—

quickly now, because soon the others will arrive
who carry sticks and guns for a living.

THE AMERICAN HOUSE OF JAZZ AND POETRY

We're all disabled here, on unemployment and welfare, afraid
of the telephone, police and bootleg records of our voices.

Nobody's quite sure what's up with the mortgage, who's
responsible for the rent, where's the broom. Perseverance,

our sweet feline, she pretend-stalks the sparrows in the yard,
they mock her and eat the fleas off her back. Blind Ulysses

walked into a stop sign, tumbled down the basement stairs
on Sunday. Two more short chords, another step or two, and

that dog would've bought it, the vet said. Still Big U
licks his bowl clean. We take out the trash in October.

The living room windows are busted from when the paper boy
used to throw his wares at the house, a photo of Bird

or JFK. Benny the Cabbie says the sound of the porch swing
can make him glad, poor heart broken so long ago, no one,

not even he, remembers her face. A jar of butterflies, fading
on the kitchen sink. Polishing his shoes on his pants' legs,

somebody, rapping the signal at the side door, singing for
a little candy. Pretty, two extra upbeats. Must be Saturday

night. It's always spring in somebody's room.

A GOODBYE TO THE GREAT SUSANNAH MCCORKLE

Let no one mislead you, she did not jump or fall, she stepped
into the air because it had become the lightest thing

for her to enter. Her life was full of imaginings, misgivings,
dreaming that by striking the earth from so far above

she could break her bones into stones, multiplying herself.
To walk out the window as a way of moving more

like liquid, to flow, incessant and strong, a final
dignity she had witnessed, other days beside the river.

She had dreamed, too, of becoming one with the tide, only
that's another way of taking on more weight. Her business

was this lightness, not a desire to fill and sink, to rise
and explode. Simply she stepped into the cool spring

air, a last hit of oxygen sweet in her lungs, trapped there,
while only her heart leaped, rapped at her chest to be free.

LULLABY

The overwrought teacher wrestles with a dream
that resembles the classroom bully. When the rhinoceros closes

to serve him up on the point of an ancient horn,
the teacher awakens late, tumbles into his pants and stumbles

down the stairs. He's got to stop keeping company
with those heavy-drinking intellectuals, and the women

they pass around like popcorn. Sure, he's a cynic,
but he's also late, an endangered species at the workplace,

and on the run from demons that chase each other in his dreams.
Scars on the road betray where this driver reached for his brake

too late. The classroom air rumbles with paper rockets
and pencil missiles. As I write this, I am late as this paper

that perhaps will take years to reach you, if ever.
I fold in the corners of this, my jet and my lullaby,

and sail an angel out over the boulevard of shadows,
one of which, I might guess from a distance, is yours.

THIS PLACE, NOW

The newspaper blown beneath the subway stairs wrestles with
the homeless man. It's easy to see which is winning. He

has good fortune, having absorbed the smell of this place and
now can sleep here unencumbered. Impossible to read

details of grief: the local woman who loses her life
when the bus in Israel is bombed, one teacher bound for

peace, which her family asks us to honor. Our Senator
proved guilty of statutory rape insists that harmless

fantasy was involved: he and a volunteer who talked
long nights on the hot telephone, from his home where his wife—

beautiful with him now on the front page—slept. How she sleeps
now we can guess for ourselves, and must guess: the story we

would read is contained in the folds of a sleeping man's arms:
twisted like hot shrapnel, formed like a monk in prayer for us.

A SEED FOUND IN AN OLD BOOK OF POEMS

Grass has begun to grow from a finger of vodka
leftover in last night's glass. A small man

floats on his back, kicks out with his feet,
either swimming or having his nightmare

in a book left open on the table.
With the rain blowing in, our young faces lifted

from between the rounded stones of the old city.
Beneath silent angels, the gargoyles frozen into position.

A man who once sold rags is fleeing. And still
the footnotes argue beside the burning river.

PRIESTS IN A CAR

Four of them, going somewhere at midnight.

I might trust them, if they wore earrings.

Keep them in front of me, when we stop at the bank.
Keep my dog at my side.

Strange white flowers, rising from black skirts,
what vicious plans behind pale foreheads.

Reminding me now of my father at the wheel, wearing his hat.

My brother is dead, at the bottom of his box.
The poison red dust, it does not wash free.

IN THE NIGHT

My father has my ear. He comes to me
in my sleep, and like coring an apple,

with his ax he has lifted my ear from
the side of my face. *Not bad*, I think,

*for a policeman, who was taught mostly
to wield a gun and a bat.* He sits late,

the ear on the plate, on the table there
before him. I join in the ranks of John

the Baptist: my father will take a piece
of my face at a time. *You false prophet,*

he says into my ear. I brush at my face,
big mosquito, I think, from the hole in

the screen. Really it's my blood running
down my cheek, my father a Gothic doctor

at work at his sink. *How much of my son
can we see in his ear?* He whispers, *Yes,*

*my dirty peach, you were our afterthought
after a long night's work.* I'm on my feet

in my dream. The cliff that I'm driven to
explodes with such startling light that I

don't hear it when my father's last bullet
blows off the rest of my face. In the night

my voice joins the chorus that sings No.

FATHER

"Father being the loneliest word
    in the one language…"
                    John Berryman

The sea across my father's face
sometimes was a mad whip.

My father's parents had the life
as immigrants, so he used the key

hidden beneath the mat: my father
was a latchkey child.

At this point in the poem
my father harbors hatred.

My father worked two jobs,
and I work to fill that hole.

I can put out many sentences
that contain the word "father,"

yet not one would feature
homemade toys. I would like

to speak man to man, or boy to boy,
whichever is best

when it comes to fathers.
My father was a policeman:

"Move along now, son…."
We are all immigrants, Father,

on the dark journey to the new world,
and some are lost along the way.

LEMONADE

Let the man who called a cement floor his resting place
dance from the memory of expensive marble.

Why waste fresh-cut flowers at a grave site
when the sweat of lovemaking might be shared?

Let's remember how she undid the buttons of a dress
one summer afternoon: there was a fly in the room,

then the children came home and made lemonade,
pits and all, which made it that much better.

Remember how the man quit his factory job,
washed off the work table, and punched the clock,

with only two words to say, " 'Night now."
Memory comes to stick or stroke us, to

bust a gut when people say "Be serious," or
to make you weep on a desolate subway platform.

What the hell. Wear the yellow shirt today. Subscribe
to a radical magazine. Send away

for a piece of the original cross,
and may you be in love on the day that you die.

Part One, II

WHO ELSE BUT THE ICE MAN

Behind a rolling ball comes the running child,
behind the running child comes the bouncing
ball. In front of a truck she meets who else but

The Ice Man. In heaven she tells God about
her school. God asks angels to look into things
in class. Amy Jacobs, as the girl had said,

is a real snob, so God sends her dreams about
the girl who was crushed by a truck. Pretty soon
Amy's grades slip, her appearance becomes, well,

"slovenly," her teacher says, and her parents
agree to counseling for the entire family,
her mother in tears and her father clearly

swinging his defensive rage like a golf club—
"Don't stand too close to someone who is this pissed,"
as he often has reminded his family.

Partners at his firm take only so much of
"this crap," telling him that he can be replaced.
Not one for ultimatums, he resigns from

"the whole broken mess," taking off with a girl
he's flirted with for months on the long commute
home, "you just out of college, and me between

homes," he laughs, in the back highway motel where
they spend their first week together. "It won't last,"
both of them think separately, but each decides

not to tell the other just yet. Amy, his
daughter whom we've nearly forgotten, dressed now
in black—fishnets, combat boots, with an earring

post through her tongue—climbs onto a Harley scooter,
a cage with yellow canaries swinging from
her right hand, her left arm wrapped around a boy

who will sneak her up to a small room he knows
above the laundromat where he had worked, "dirty,
but with the noise of the machines, they can't hear

worth shit," and there they will stay until they can't.
Amy carries the purple notebook she stole
from the convenience store, "'cause stealing's *so cool*,"

along with the twelve cans of chunk light tuna
that she was able to stuff into her pack.
She's only begun to use her new notebook,

with no idea where stories like this can go,
yet she thinks she's got the beginning down pat:

"Behind a rolling ball comes a running child.
Behind a running child comes the bouncing
ball. In front of a truck she meets who else

but The Ice Man."

THE GIRL, THE DOG, AND THE BOOK

A girl is riding on the back of a dog.
In his mouth, the dog is carrying a book,
on the first page of which, a girl is riding

on the back of a dog. As the story goes,
it's the dog who chose the girl, and she's held on
ever since. Her small hands tighten with handfuls

of short hair. The world, a cool place, blurred forms,
colors that fly by as they ride, and the girl
has made a home for the wind in her hair. She

wears no clothes, and the dog, huge dark energy
beneath her, his panting like the pumping
of her heart. The dog, for a moment, larger

than a mountain, the girl, hugging a hair, lost
in the woods on his back. She builds a house, starts
her fire, brings the dog back down to size. She sleeps

in a cavity, in the corner of his mouth, swimming
in and out, from the white page to the yellow stones
of his teeth. White foam rises, warm waves breaking

all around her. She spins herself a great nest,
cocoon woven from her long hair. And inside,
a girl is riding on the back of a dog.

In his mouth, the dog is carrying a book,
over the first pages, the girl's hands rapidly moving.

MOTHER AND FATHER FIRE

Spark, then fire begins. Fire pulls oxygen
deep into the box. *Come, child, there's something
I'd like to show you in the back of this
iron box.* Fire inhales, huffs, and spits

more fire. Startled awake, a spider is killed.
The curious child is drawn deeper in
as the fire says kind things like *Home is red*
and *Yellow is the color of love,* so

the child becomes more familiar as she
begins to pat the fire, to name it *Good
Sir,* think of it as a kind dog. Walls rise
around the child, the fire is all tongues

for her. It licks the knee that she scraped
at play, nests in her hair the way gentle
birds will at dawn. Climbing up until she
can look straight into the eye of the fire,

the child asks that the fire sing the new song
for her. But the fire only beats and huffs,
slaps out the refrain that it knows the best:
Come, child, there's something I'd like to show you

here in the back of this box. The child cries
herself to sleep, her tears make the great smoke
that is her bed, and the great smoke carries
the child back up into the tree, where she

dreams her dream of Mother and Father Fire.

THE HISTORY OF BASEBALL

I'm up against Chinua Achebe.
In my dream he unquestionably is
the greatest pitcher in the world.

He has merged with Gabriel García Márquez,
I'm stepping up to the plate, he's wiping
the sweat onto his sleeve, kicking the dust

on the mound. A flock of geese passes
overhead. Achebe, Márquez, Umberto
Eco it now says on his pinstripes,

pauses with me as we watch. "They are
English geese," he tells me. "It's their time
for tea." Now that we're side by side, I see

the eyes belong to Anne Sexton. Nobody has
dark wells like these. We are close enough
to kiss, she looks at me and says, "I could

reach inside you and pull out a small bone,
without disturbing that toy smile on your face."
I'm back at the plate, with my strategy

to bow each time the pitcher delivers.
A thin string of fire runs from my face
to the face of the figure sweating on the mound.

Each time I bow, I pull in a little light.

THE COMPLETE WORKS

Somewhere before the 10,000 chimpanzees
finish typing the complete works of Shakespeare,
they will have typed this poem.

The cow that jumped over the moon
will appear before the dissociative babble,
the lunacy of Ophelia, her love

like so many petals, a mad penny tossed
into the sea, wishing back her father
the fool. Again our Prince lunges, finally

to kill the rat typed into hiding
behind the bedroom curtain. A misplaced comma,
where you would have met the love of your life;

and where a kiss, or the word Yes might be uttered,
a chimp screams for a forgotten thing in the forest.

NEAR AND DISTANT NEIGHBORS

When the mother who screams into his face is away,
the young Sámi boy in the bedroom above me sings.
A stray, Norwegian elk hound visits the back door. He
cowers when I bend to set a bowl of table scraps

in the snow. He would dive beneath the arctic ice cover
if he could, three patient weeks before he allows me
to place my palm beneath his face. Another man somewhere
has beaten him. Behind a tightly sealed window, there

barely parting the curtain, a little spy peers out
on me, out for my walk, aurora borealis above.
Pause, read what the night scribbles against the dark sky,
linger, between languages, and watch the light with a boy.

MY LOVE FOR YOU

(before you saw this page, before the water
of my fear broke, through New England winters,
the loneliness, when my dead ones came
to teach me the lessons—sent large packages

to my soul, scratched my initials
into tombstones, spent months without visiting
my dreams, and when they came all they said
was "Well then?") is intense.

THIS SOLITUDE

I sit in the Thin Man Café,
say an original prayer into my plate of rice.

I've spoken to the silent roaches,

have cried over the nearness of a warm tomato.

I have plans to rinse my stiff cold hands
under the squirt of milk from a cow's full udder.

My feet tell the story of the streets
where I've fled,

seeking solace from the man
with the gold face and the iron cane.

I'm a hunter, I am sticking out my tongue.

I pray to be struck by lightning.

THE SLEEPERS

When the soldiers had come
casting their wet dice against the shithouse wall,
gambling for parts of my body
and cutting me to pieces
(how hungry they were),

When the militia arrived
burying me up to my neck in the sand,
setting my hair on fire
so that they could read the faces
of village girls who came down to dance,

When the infantry had settled down
for a dusty night, and it was ordained for me
to work my tongue bloody on their boots,
each star in the sky
coming up clear red on the leather,

every best friend I'd ever had
slept soundly in a white feather bed.

BOY WHO CRIED WOLF

There's no excusing it,
they should have gone
when he came blowing his whistle,
shaking his little ball head
like a bell in that small tower.
That last time
with the secret in his fist,
waving it and letting it go
like a familiar red balloon.
In the village sleephouse,
the butcher's hands
were two hairy animals,
balled up for the winter,
the constable far gone
behind his intolerable, iron teeth.
Grandma and Mother slept deep
in their wolf clothes.
As many of these
as there are knives in the week.
The child on the hill.
In the morning,
greeting the sun,
sheepless.

THE NAME

In memory of Anne Sexton

They said her name, let us say Anne.
Her name was being said.
It was that time.
Her name was round, it became sharp,
a drop of water falling.
It was the name,
we were all saying it then.
The name grew larger, let's say
bigger than the town we came from.
No, it seems to me now,
a name as large as the town,
which, when written, gathered like clouds.
The letters came together—
with their movements and directions
they were like monuments—
to cover and to copy every street.
Nothing, no one, remained untouched.
Every one of us lived under the name.
The name descended on us like night,
it included our hate and love and ignorance.

The world is no longer large enough,
the name has moved on.
The day will come when they will say your name.
And, when it covers us, there we will sleep.

NOTES OF A GREAT EXECUTIVE

Oh, I baked beans with my stare.
My jargon opened windows
from which lesser men would jump.
I grew like corn in my heyday
and rode off into the sunset
before it was popular to do that.
I was born on a ship slotted for sinking,
and I sailed it around the world.
My cargo was fever; I cut its throat
with the feathers of laughter.
When I was two, I sold my grandmother.
She could sew like the wind,
so she fetched a fair price.
By age four I had the largest paper route
in Detroit. I delivered your paper
while the lines were warm as bread.
Before crimes were committed,
I collected rewards. Before criminals
were born, I had their mothers arrested
in howling, maternity-ward lineups.
I was really cute when I was ten
and way ahead of my time.
I disappeared from milk cartons
and hid in the Nevada desert,
where I discovered nuclear power.
A quack of a physicist made the bomb
from formulas found in my trash.
I bottled and marketed cactus juice.
To prove I had a sense of humor,
I had myself crucified. I survived
without much squawking. The birds
of paradise drape me in fine linen;
I will rise no later than Sunday. The great
nest of stories multiplies under their beaks.
Break this bread, friend, and pass it along.

KEVIN'S BODY

A dark, beautiful furniture. River
pulled in every direction. Your knuckles

thinly disguised stones on their way
back to this earth. Your head alone

a remarkable egg. What will come
of you, the wind turning the page,

scattered among the night animals?

BE NOT AFRAID

I was raised by people with stones in their pockets.
I walked down streets that were curling tongues of flame.

The green grocer held his small wet knife to my throat,
the butcher popped delicate cubes of meat from the small

of my back. His stew drew a dozen hungry thieves
in the evening. They stole my breath, they shaved the hair

from my entire body, and told me I would never
sing. Be not afraid. The trees they dropped on my back

have not crushed my spine, I have brought back the bowl
from which they made me eat glass, and I have learned

this new dance now.

Part Two, I

THE MEN WHO KILLED MY BROTHER

Behind the left ear a scar
shaped like the hand of a priest lifted

to bestow a blessing, a small
neat mustache like many men

standing in a row, where
you, me, a friend's sister

might point and say *That one*, and from there
his right to remain silent

began. The second carried himself
like a boat far from water, too

large for a man, the size of an average
desk turned on its side. My memory

makes him a lover of pizza, sour cream and butter
plopped down and running

from a potato, that vegetable shape
not unlike his own. The third I would have

a drained green bottle, a cracked
clay pot with begonias, the anonymous

tan ruler made of cheap pine—shape, voice,
texture and odor

beyond my knowing, my extended
day in the desert, my mind a violent

sea before the calm. Living,
and suffering like my brother, Murderers,

have I forgotten
to thank or to forgive you?

DRIVE

The long drive toward New York
when my brother was killed,
thrown to the cement
of an elevator floor.

I flew down the freeway
through Connecticut,
lead foot on the accelerator
until my tears choked
what little vision remained,
until I saw,
no matter how fast I flew,
I could not turn back time.

I coasted into the breakdown lane
and aimed the car
at the last lights that came clear,
the twenty-foot-tall red letters
of the Ramada Inn. The letters
crawl like a fire
on the windshield. It rains
as if the Son of God has been killed.

The woman who made the trip with me
had arrived at my place,
sat me at the kitchen table
and knelt at my feet,
as if knowing and praying
that I would not follow him.

Before departure, I destroy the bedroom door
with my fists, my blood
begging angels of death to pass over.

I insisted I needed to drive,
to hold, or caress and feel,

something tangible,
to hold on to the wheel
as I hold on to this pen,
as a way of holding on
to life itself, to push it forward
when it will not go on its own.

As a way of groping forward,
I drank a quart of gin
and my friend and I had sex
somewhere during our trip.
I have no idea
where she is today,
yet I send this flier out
with gratitude, for she grieved
my grief with me. Then
she continued to drive us
toward the family that waits
around our large dining room table.

Death is incomplete
until the brother arrives
who lives furthest away.

He is still falling for me,
and I am driving on to see him,
as long as someone is reading this book.

NOTES ON OUR BEASTLY NATURE

My sister's boyfriend taught me to eat french fries
with my fingers. "Forks are for people," he said.
"We're more like animals." Once, awakened from

a sound sleep, I found my rug savagely gnawed
and frayed, dew of the forest under my arms,
the scent of some wild thing around my genitals.

My nails were cracked, fingers muddy and bleeding.
I know now that my middle name is Beast.
I stand tall to make the necessary sounds

among people, to do my best not to go
home alone, where I would curse the unkind stars
for loneliness. The evolutionary wand

takes me by surprise. I feel like a plant
at computer terminals and complex machines.
We diminish, and we die: the grandmother,

with one breast, who fed me chocolate on the sly,
the train that smoked around the tree late Decembers,
the goldfish I ignored that week I discovered girls.

DIALECTIC

Sister Florence wanted to know
what freedom meant. "Freedom means,"
I replied, not timid to speak
at first, "doing what you want."
"What you *want*," she barked back,
the strained emphasis on 'want'
meant that was the word
I was to change, the irrevocable dialogue
now begun. "Freedom means doing what
you think is right." "What you *think*
is right," the mad nun now targeted
the new word to be changed. Years later
I would learn to call this method
Dialectic; it was dated and painful. "Freedom,"
the very thing I felt diminishing
as Sister Florence closed the distance
between us, "is doing what's right."
"And if you thought it was right
to throw Mr. D'Angelo out the window,
you would be free to do it?" Sure,
I thought. Bring Chet D'Angelo
into this. Chet never slept well.
His bedroom door hung on one hinge,
and his mother stayed up drinking,
with one guy or another, or doing wash
under a sixty-watt bulb. It dangled
from a string in their kitchen, burning
all the hours of the night, so notes home
did little good. Every chance in school
the nuns pulled Chet into classroom
"discussions," as they nicknamed
this guessing-game form of torture,
or they pushed themselves into Chet's
tiny, flood-lit dreams. "Freedom,"
I said, feeling sad for Chet and
wanting to free him from the hook,

"is doing what you're supposed to do,
what you and the priests tell us
to do, and what the Bible says."
Now, pulling in the net of their lies,
feeling like a lawyer, I smiled.
"And if I told you to throw
Mr. D'Angelo out the window?"
This is when Chet raised his head
from his desk-top nap, said,
"Sister, did you call me by name?"
and every sixth-grader laughed so loud
that someone passing in the hall might hear,
so old Florence got embarrassed. She called
Chet to the front of the room, squared off
and hauled a roundhouse slap at his face.
But with the instinct of a boxer
just awakened by a bell, Chet ducked
and reached in with a left jab
to sting the right side of her face,
enough that four red fingers
appeared there ten minutes later.
Twenty-eight small hearts stopped beating,
except for the gorilla bomb in the chest
of that nun. Then Chet ran out,
toward the signs that say Emergency and Exit,
and you could hear his small feet
beat steady time down the hall, the sound
diminishing and the echo growing,
until he reached the crash bar
of that last door, clipped it
with a crisp *ca-chunk*, our quiet room filling
with D'Angelo's intense conclusion.

NO, EDWARD

In eighth-grade, Sister Ellen Mary asked me,
"What's happened to you, Edward?" This meant
many things to me: to my friends I was
Ed, what my grandfather's friends called him;
to the basketball team and the boys with whom
I had begun to smoke pot, I was Big Ed; to the girls
who were then beginning to grow breasts, I was
Eddie, the form of my name which terrified me
because their bodies left me not knowing
what to do, and with no excuses. My mother alone
called me Edward, which struck me as strangely
coincidental that both she and Ellen Mary handled me with
similar formal stiffness and starch, and they never smiled.
Precisely what that nun wanted to know was why,
when she walked into our homeroom that morning,
was I standing up at the blackboard,
holding the globe on my head and singing,
"He's got the whole world on his head"
to the eighth-grade class. "This is Africa,"
I pointed to the underbelly of the globe,
trying to convince Ellen Mary she had caught me
in the middle of some ad-lib geography lesson.
But already she had seen eighteen years of youth
being trained to do their Catholic tricks,
so I hung my head because obviously the jig
was up, and I put the globe down on the desk.
Then she did exactly the wrong thing. She said,
"No, Edward. Hold that globe there where you held it,
and walk the hallway until you hear the bell
for lunch." This made me the most popular kid
in grammar school. By that moment in eighth-grade—
when I first unfolded my fingers, perhaps the first sign
that I was saying goodbye to my God,
then reached to her desk to grab the globe
and hold it on my head—already I had decided
that was the day their Edward was to die
because I'd had enough of going unnoticed in the world.

WITNESS

"Is God a memory or a presence?" I would
guess 'memory,' what with all the old
stories in the Bible, but the priest already
looks at me sternly, and I wonder
whether he would pound me
should my guess prove to be wrong.
The man has a reputation for breaking
unbreakable combs, whenever a boy adjusts
his hair in a classroom. The priest leans
on his breviary, and the old oak table
built by Vermont monks, from a time when
the parish had the money to send away
for nice, handmade things. The altar,
which stretches on invisible outside
the closed doors of our private lesson,
in the sprawling Byzantine half-light
of the cathedral-like church, is made
of imported marble, an Italian gift
from the father of one of the original
nuns, her name preserved in memoriam
along the bottom edge of a huge
stained-glass window, all of it shipped
to America, piece by costly piece. "The Church
is Holy," the priest reminds me, as I
squirm in my seat, and he pushes his fingers
forward, as if they were a flower blossoming
right there in my face. I can hear
the tall, wide metal doors yawn
out of sight, the rush-hour traffic roaring
for a moment on the boulevard, where the boy
would like to be headed home, the sounds,
like people caught in the background
of a photograph, then the particular sound
of a woman's hard heels, her short steps
on the mosaic marble inlay that leads her
toward the altar. "Sacred Heart of Jesus,"

she calls. "You take my husband. Why you no
take me, too?" The priest holds a finger up
to his lips, silencing himself and calling
me to this communion of witness, the woman's
broken language like a scarred record
playing the same phrases again and again.
He places his large hand, easily covering
all my folded fingers— "this the church, this
the steeple, open the doors, and see all
the people"—stopping my only avenue for
the great reserve of energy I had gathered
forever in the front left row, where seated
alphabetically I would learn the lessons
of the kingdom, the power, and the glory.

SCIENCE CLASS

I was there the day Father Svec
slapped Eric Silkowski, my second cousin,
up and down the length of the hallway
because Eric had said "Fuck"
to Mrs. Hlubik. The lesson, that day
in science class, had nothing to do
with procreation or copulation, and Eric
had made use of the direct object
"you," a simple, strange combination uttered
from the back of seventh-grade. "Eric?"
Odd, that day, how she had used his name
as interrogative, yet for an elastic moment
the boy himself had earned the integrity
of a question. "You heard me," followed
his steady, slow declarative statement.
I remember two key insights from
the entire, seventh-grade science class:
to determine whether a "shampoo scrub"
is necessary, one needs to scratch
the scalp with a fingernail, then
to sniff the nail. I can see her,
holding her fingernail to her flared
nostril. The second bit of wisdom was that
we must feed "our little friends," as she
referred to the sparrows, but not others
that migrate, and always to take care
because feeding birds can bring rats
in the city. Mrs. Hlubik still stands
there at her desk, and after blinking twice
and pursing her lips, she marches out
into the hall and to the classroom
next-door. With closed eyes you can hear
them loudly whispering: the priest's
urgent questions, their rapid and rising
banter that follows the short telling
of her story. The dark form seconds later

appears at the doorway, inviting Eric
into the hallway, where he might repeat
what he had said. The long black dress
is stark below the man's pale, balding head,
the same who would be sent to another parish
because of the wild "rumors" sprouting,
the serious boundaries he had crossed
with altar boys. It seems the world is built
on stories, like the one the priest himself
had told in sex education: how older boys
on his school football team had included him
in an intimate circle, and had taught him there
how to masturbate. The sky is darkening
around me, growing dense with the idea
of a heavy March rain, the arc of a story
worth nothing if it's not told. Leaning
on a mailbox, a quiet Back Bay neighborhood,
I am scribbling on receipts, battered postcards
from old friends, paused at this place where
what stays calls me to remember. An old woman
taps at her living room window, she waves
her hand, as if at a fly, for me to go away
from her house. I hear the priest's insistent
questioning, "What did you say? What?"—
the swish of his long gown, the powerful
repetitive clap of his open palm on the boy's
terrified face, the same that might be handled
more affectionately another day—how reluctant
the boy had been to go into the hall—and still
Mrs. Hlubik standing there in front, simply
keeping watch over the sheep, and me thinking,
for you, Eric: *All right. I'll go. Fuck you.*

3:15

Delicate, this time of day, when the boy owns
his own body, walking alone down the boulevard,

clad in a stupid, blue Catholic school blazer,
some saint's initials in gold on the tie. Dead

the saint, the nuns, the priests, and the parents,
nobody still alive but this one boy's wings

beating autumn leaves down to golden powder. *Yes*
to the grasshopper, to the brown crap that he spits

into my palm. *Whatever you say*, to the old lady
who runs out with a butter knife, still chewing bread,

the same she baked in Europe, swearing that she'll cut
my little white throat, *You little son of a bitch,*

because I've trapped a bee in one of her pink roses
and have ripped it from the vine. *Yes*, unmurdered me,

my cherry blood and my young ship of bone.

THE FAMILY SEWER

Ostensibly: that place where the putrid waters
would gather, steel as hard as the stuff
from which they make thin razors and swift swords,

how many eyeholes that my father had drilled
so that strong, acid rains carrying diesel blue,
lead from gasoline, would have a place to flow,

a dark hole leading toward a tunnel that would kill
water spiders, the young fish testing the currents,
north Jersey run-off sure to work its way

from dilapidated garages in a backyard, small
car houses that leaned like pale, green beasts
into the middle of a gone century—away

from the pavement to creep back insidiously
into the soil, where a hapless fool plants his tree,
a tomato for hope, a large, oddly purpled fruit

that stings and bites back when it first hits
your tongue—gone, the days when the father now old,
weathered, fried and bent over like a streetlight,

would send a bad boy to stand on a steel plate
under the slow curve, the steady curse of the sun,
that terrible jewel sailing so far above

the small planet, and the tiny boy, siblings
circling and taunting like cruel satellites
on their bicycles, and the mother watching

silent, exhaling smoke from her kitchen window,
still, for hours, my damned goddess of wild waters.

Part Two, II

DEVOTED

It's a Sunday, and my eyes are burning
like those smoky, little votive candles

they always told you you could light for someone,
say a prayer, and it would matter. But never

the whole one-hundred-fifty times I walked
Susan Rondholz home from school would she kiss me,

her skirt a little shorter than the rest,
as I remember them now, really nice legs,

navy blue school uniform socks pulled to her knees.
It did no good, my mother smoking on the porch,

holding the dog's leash as if no animal
were attached to it, blankly staring away

straight through heavy traffic. No kind word,
no What did you learn in school today? maybe

a quick shot from her eyes, two small, iron rods
fixing me, tearing me down with that beam

of a stare. I know all about you, her
wordless pursed lips could say. Despite my prayers,

my policeman father came home day after day,
never pinned beneath a truck, never cut down

by one of those dark, dangerous people
he always told us about when he asked you

to pass the goddamn eggplant, and don't you
dare waste those lima beans. People elsewhere

were starving, and there was a war to fight.
Why don't you stop it? I asked, on the little

stiff red kneeler, using a quarter I'd swiped
from my mother's purse. She would never miss

what there would never be enough of anyway,
and a little change, to stop a war or get

a touch of affection, I couldn't see what
this just God was waiting for. Still, our boys,

strange how they dragged themselves back, one by one,
as it sure seemed we were losing our

great battle for freedom. Our house hung
with a banner when the neighbor's son upstairs

came back as a stranger, looked at my body,
then at my face, nodding once as if to say,

You can pray all you want, some things have changed,
and not only your voice.

YOUTH IN JERSEY CITY

Every corner had ones like us,
wherever we met we fought,
played basketball or made friends,
friends that would or wouldn't stay.

We thieved, stealing what wasn't
bolted into place: fire hydrants for the new
streets near the projects, selling them back
to the corrupt power and water company.

We tore pipes from city buildings
at night: selling the copper
for scrap. Pound for pound it bought us
a taste of honey, reefer, and containers of beer.

We plotted the schedules of police,
watching their homes and noting vacations,
busting in, taking their weapons, their wives' jewels,
while they sunned themselves in Antigua and Jamaica.

They shot us unarmed in the back,
we shot them face-first when we could.
They taught us what were the delicate
pouches, the fragile sticks in our bodies:

breaking each, with joy in their faces,
rolling us down hills and hanging us
from spiked fences, abusing our girlfriends
because they were evil men, lacking authentic love.

Nearly a code among us, how we hated
our parents. They bred into us an expert
malignancy. Some of us, grown older and stronger,
would return the favor with a baseball bat.

We gave back to the earth, the city,
a higher percentage than the Bible asks
for charity. Of those who survived a third
were sent to fight for Sam in foreign lands.

Some number of us would never return,
others would bring back the pieces, a full
ripe fruit, for the streets and the prisons.
I've fled from my friends, a quiet side street,

far north from the warriors and the battle.
A car door startles, a crow is threatening,
I'm at my desk, writing for my life:
watching the bolted door, holding a pen, my knife.

FIRE ESCAPE

so hot that my face was melting
in the glass that had become viscous
looking into the kitchen
of the third-floor apartment. I'd spent
the morning with a wire brush
working my knuckles bloody between
wrought iron leaves and bars that curled
and swerved. Tar on the garage roof below
undulated, a word beyond reach
that fierce, August heat wave, a spindly
and dirty sumac climbing out
of the sewer, all my limbs shooting
past the broken glass that surrounded me
with its stellar sweetness, amber and green
constellations gone bad, yellow jackets
intent on my eyes, squinting to free a speck
of rust caught in one corner, my vision
compromised, no longer a stereo view
of the world. I pushed aluminum cans
aside in my wake, coiled and snaked
as best a boy could
amidst the traffic of my father's
rage and hate. "Drink the sun,"
he said, when I spoke
of thirst, a bad-mood day
for an overworked Dad. But I'm not making
any excuse. A neighbor played
the forgiving god that day, a tall
cold glass of tea, when she peeked out
to water her plants, absent tomatoes
she knew I had stolen and smashed
in the dark the night before.

WHAT THERE WAS

There was the annoyance of
someone in the other room
eating a crisp apple,
a woman's heels on the stairs.
The door slammed, my father's
black shoes gone for night work,
each of his fifteen steps
adding strength to my wings
until I flew into the night.

There were bells at dawn from the church
opposite Mosquito Park, where abandoned men,
biting at the air, huddled together
like one silent machine, over a fire
raging in a barrel. The milk trucks
and the paper deliveries clanked
down Kennedy Memorial Boulevard, and wove
through that city's filthy side streets
after the wreckage of a Saturday night.

We were the students asleep like beggars
on the floors of friends or strangers—
faces heavy with lipstick,
swollen from so much booze,
from the hardball of all-night party.
Our hands were black from searching
the night that never would answer.
We all wore black, but not one of us
dreamed that death was unbeatable.

BRINGING THE DOG BACK

Because of its dependence on her,
my mother loved our dog like a son.
The dog died at one-thirty a.m.
the morning after Christmas,
of tremendous importance to my mother
because she wanted the dog
to see Christmas to its end.
When he quaked and whimpered
in the culmination of pain so great
that we nearly died watching him,
Mother consented finally
to put the dog far from its misery
and ours. Our acceptance had come
weeks before, each suffering whine of the dog
followed by a sideways glance
at our mother, waiting for her to say,
"The dog's time has come."

The animal hospital was open all night,
forty-five minutes from where we lived
in Jersey City. My father and I
piled the animal in blankets,
and in painful yelps it registered
every bump of the New Jersey roadway.
I cried over that bastard of a dog,
partly because it made me feel
that I was one more piece in the board game
invented by my mother. She had accepted
my brothers and me as published fact,
so when my brother was killed early
that next April in New York, addicted
and wanted in three states, she shared
not a single public tear. Yet I remember
how she wailed in such sadness when,
two days before the dog died
of her final choice, it fell,

legs splayed like clay animation,
in front of our apartment. Hearing her scream
a pain which I had heard
never before in life, I rushed outside.
But she met me halfway, in the hall, where
repeatedly she punched my chest, screaming
between her hysterical sobs of motherhood,
"Get out there, you bastard,
and bring that dog back to me."

EXILED FROM NEW JERSEY

I wanted to come back, Brother, and visit
your grave. They should have buried you in the park
where, one dark night, you mugged an old man and wore
his Yankee cap until morning, when, beneath a tree, police
arrested your nearly frozen, stoned-out body. Saved
by the very men who beat you. Ironic after
years of having been beaten by our father the cop, to
have teeth chipped and ribs cracked by our father
in more universal numbers. Seasons recur, the calendar
year alone is linear. I march around the house,
what I do for a living. They won't let me back in
New Jersey. The bridges, the tunnels, the turnpike
posted with pictures of my face. The world is now
a post office bulletin board. I am wanted
without being desired. You're good and frozen
now, old buddy. The thermometer dipped down
late last night, the low hours of my mind, the ground
solid as a stopped clock. Your heart must be strangely
broken down by now, every artery collapsed, the scar,
where you once nearly lost your life, faded, neatly folded,
a creased, ten-year-old map I can't look at. Travel by car
makes my heart punch in its frightened cage. Everyone I know
now has never met you. From where you are sleeping,
the spring after you had died, I saw the Twin Towers, two-
dimensional, a married couple flat in the distance,
looking over all their little children, all of their
tiny streets—the pushcarts driven by Chinese, the beaten-
faced prostitutes, pores in their faces that you could
fall into, the old, Central Park horses in the rain,
feed bags secure, a pile of crap behind each. The Towers
weeping their big glass windows over the city, huddled
each to keep the other from the rain, and you
so deadly silent. How literal my mind has become.
Exiled from New Jersey, I wander, I tear at my beard.
I will walk without shoes each of the million streets.

WHY DON'T THE CHILDREN CALL ANYMORE

Mother clenches her teeth
while she sleeps. Black and white
houses chase her. She hides
in the forest, terrified
that her son has been captured
and is now held prisoner
somewhere in New England.
What does this mean
to her? Father wonders,
leaning above her
to count the rapid eye
movement. *She is obviously*
pursued by something, tremendously
black, and more white
than I've ever seen. Father
retrieves his .38
from the dresser drawer. Carefully,
he undoes her fist
and fits the gun
into her palm. *Protection,*
he thinks, *against whatever*
is inside. Mother is exhausted
most mornings, and Father pleads
that she see someone. "I see
things all the time," she says,
reaching across the table
to hand him the warm gun.
"What have you done
with the bodies?" Father asks.
"I've taken them back,"
Mother replies. "They were mine
to begin with."

HAPPY BIRTHDAY, TOMMY MURPHY

Yesterday was May 5, and again I remembered a pal
I used to have in Jersey City, Tommy Murphy, whose birthday
falls on the 5th of May, exactly a month after mine, and who
was in love with my younger sister, Grace, something which
he confessed to me with appropriate solemnity, a sort of
life-or-death seriousness that we placed on such disclosures
in our late teens and early twenties, an attitude which, on
my best days, I can at least halfway emulate today. Finnbar—
a name by which our half of the city knew him, his irresistible
middle name, which shouted out for us to use it—somehow
never made it happen with my little sister, only a year younger
than Finnbar himself, as much a young woman as he
was a man, as attractive to him as his middle name was
to us. His pining away for her lasted maybe a year-
and-a-half, and I can see the two of them there, leaning on
the fence that belonged to Richie Geiger, our neighbor
whose shadow my brother-in-law once saw, as the man
crouched on the roof of the apartment building next-door:
the silhouette of a man with a rifle—a BB gun, the truth
that would come clear later—moving slightly, like a stiff
branch from a strong, internal wind, as he searched adjacent
roofs and yards through a scope, a laid-off postal worker
shooting pigeons in his spare time. Geiger didn't like it,
his son dancing for money at gay clubs in New York City, but
what father would, and who could tell if this had anything to do
with his killing of birds? And then who could trust *him*, my
brother-in-law, a Viet Nam Veteran who once tossed a large
table-model television from his third-floor apartment window
because he said the bad screen held too many memories? It was
cocaine, finally, that claimed Fat Mike, paranoid and dragged
from the apartment he had shared with my older sister
for thirteen years—such a bad TV show, those gorilla-like
swat men descending on the bulk that was Fat Mike, more
muscle than flab, daunting, even as he sat there placid
in his favorite rocker. Whatever happened to Richie Geiger
rested with the courts, and Finnbar, safe from fast-moving

clouds overhead, the flying TVs and the shadows of men, leans
lightly on the fence in my mind—what better place for him, even if
memory is a prison—that summer day that he worked to say
whatever was not right or enough.

ROOSEVELT STADIUM

The city stopped the summer concerts there
after a boy we knew named Guy had his throat cut
with a broken bottle. YES played that night,
"In and Around the Lake," "Long Distance
Run-around," yet we never got in
to see the show. Had his throat cut while wearing
a Brothers of the Jersey City Heights'
tee-shirt. Once word reached us, my brother Matt
turned his inside-out, we scalped our tickets
and beat it out of there. There were 385
of us Brothers, a worthy, not-too-shabby number
for a good-sized city. Fights between neighborhoods
qualified as riots. At nineteen, when the lure of gangs
had gone from me, I returned to where the tall weeds
smelled of garbage, a life gone by, and mixed it up there
with a girl named Michele. She swore that it beat the hell
out of a smelly motel room, each of us surprised that the other
expected to be on top. How she punched my chest
when she came, while something, a small rat maybe,
scampered by my long hair in the grass. I couldn't care
less, let the thing leap for my jugular, the memory
of a dead boy shoot through my mind. I screamed as much
for him as for her, noble under the blows
that she rained down on me. Other nights she tore
the skin on my back, sent me home sore with a blood-stained
tee-shirt. Twenty years, and I still lick, I bite, my mouth waters
over the memory. I was raised in the middle of one long
battle. I've put down the weapons, the bottle. Yet I know
what it means to be a lover and a warrior.